Leaders are best when p
they exist, not so good v   _ p~~p..~
acclaim them, worst when they despise
them, but of a good leader who talks little,
when their work is done, their aim
fulfilled, their people will all say "we did
this ourselves".

From Lao-Tse, Ancient Chinese Philosopher

1

A
STRAIGHTFORWARD
GUIDE
TO
EFFECTIVE
LEADERSHIP

PHILIP LEISH
STRAIGHTFORWARD PUBLISHING

Straightforward Publishing Limited
38 Cromwell Road Walthamstow
London E17 9JN

© Straightforward Publishing 1997

ISBN 1899926 06 X

Printed by BPC Wheaton Limited, Exeter

Cover design by Straightforward Graphics

Whilst every effort has been taken to ensure that the information
contained in this book is accurate at the time of printing, the author and
the publisher accept no liability for errors or omissions.

A Straightforward Guide to Effective Leadership

CONTENTS

INTRODUCTION

This book is not solely about what makes a good leader. It is not only about different theories of leadership. Too many books adopt this approach and do not begin to approach the different areas of the operating environment in which a leader must be successful in order to be called an effective leader.

Therefore, the stance this book adopts is one of initially exploring leadership and management generally but then moving on quite rapidly to the leader as a manager within the team, within a task orientated environment and the leader as decision taker, delegator, communicator, and, ultimately effective leader in an organisation.

When discussing organisations it is the medium to large organisation to which I refer.

The list of topics explored is not exclusive, there are many aspects to management and leadership. However, these central tenets have been approached and the goal of the book is to open the mind of the reader to those areas.

The approach is very much a managerial approach because that is what the book deals with- Managers in a work environment. I believe that this is the most fruitful approach because it is one that most leaders can relate to. Although there are many different leadership situations, it is the work environment which is concentrated on.

The central thesis is that leaders are not "born" are not only "natural" but can effectively develop into true leaders once a knowledge of the dynamics of the workplace has been attained.

There are many pressures on today's managers, expectancies that managers show vision and lead their teams to success. However, there are also pressures to achieve bottom lines and this can sometimes detract from the overall process of effective leadership.

The true leader is a person who can keep sight of all the processes, the tasks, the direction of the team and the position of the individual. Courage, strength and integrity must be shown, along with decisiveness and willpower. However, in addition to all the classic leadership qualities, a true leader is also a sensitive being who can effectively appraise a situation and take corrective action when necessary.

It is hoped that this book, with its emphasis on management, the team, the individual and the processes involved in leadership in a work environment, will be of use to all of those who wish to be effective leaders.

MANAGERS AND LEADERS

CHAPTER ONE

MANAGEMENT AND LEADERSHIP GENERALLY

There are a number of general theories about leadership and leaders. However, in the context of this book, we will need to look more closely at the process of management and leadership in order to understand the true dynamics of the *manager as leader*.

Leadership is not simply about telling others what to do. Many seem to think this and succeed in creating resentment and hostility in those around them. In order to understand the true qualities of a leader, the desired outcomes of leadership and to make sense of the different contexts in which leadership can be exercised, we need to first look at management generally.

It is not good enough for managers to operate on the basis of rule by fear. We live now in an age of communication and our work environments are changing rapidly. There is almost a sense of schizophrenia within people in the workplace in many organisations. There is also quite often a sense of cynicism.. On one hand managers rush around using buzzwords such as "investors in people" and "lets get the most out of our workforce" and at the same time seek to coerce others into doing what they are told. No wonder the workforce think that the reality never changes and all the efforts of managers are really for their own self gratification.

The leader of people can help to foster an environment where all are working for the good of others and at the same time are looking to leaders for inspiration. This is called *having vision and sharing it.* Creating a sense of common purpose. To achieve this the management and leadership skills of others in a managerial position must be identified and utilised.

LEADERSHIP AND MANAGEMENT

Managers jobs tend to break down into three skill areas: Technical, administrative and the achievement of results through people.

Technically, the manager must have sufficient expertise, or competence to know what to expect from others. It is not always necessary for the manager to be technically excellent but that person should be able to recognise competence in others. Administratively, it is essential to understand the procedures of ones own organisation and to maintain those procedures. Achieving results through people is where we begin to separate the leaders from the managers. The Chief executive of British

Aerospace has stated "Leadership is the art of getting more from people than they think they are capable of giving".

Developing the last skill area, the achievement of results through people, we need to look a little more closely at the person who is trying to achieve the results and also to identify leadership abilities in terms of qualities or traits of individuals, situations and functions.

QUALITIES OR TRAITS OF A LEADER

Any group of people, or team of people will expect leaders to have certain defined qualities. Obviously, these qualities will differ with each individual. A typical list, however, would be:

Courage-a leader needs to be seen as courageous and strong willed, willing to make the final decision and stand by that decision;

Willpower-the power to impose if necessary;

Initiative-this is a definite quality and a leader cannot be seen as a leader unless that person can exercise initiative;

Knowledge-a leader must be knowledgeable;

Integrity-the moment a person is seen or perceived as having a lack of integrity then that person diminishes in others eyes. As a result that persons leadership qualities also diminish;

Fitness-a person must be perceived to be physically healthy and fit;

Team spirit-if team spirit is lacking then a Person is perceived as being selfish-which is the opposite of a leader.

Obviously, the above are not rigid and any attempt to be absolutely prescriptive about a leader and leadership qualities is impossible. However, the above are good guidelines and it is easy to see that if one or more qualities are missing then a persons currency as a leader is diminished, or can be diminished.

It could be the case that a person who has certain of the above qualities may be better suited to one type of organisation than another. For example, different qualities may be required for an army officer than a senior manager in the public sector.

THE SITUATIONAL APPROACH

There are several schools of thought when ascribing qualities to leaders. One such school is that of the situationist. One approach of this school is based on recruiting a leader most suited to the situation. A natural leader can arise through a group or team or can be appointed to a post.

Leaders must certainly have the technical know how and competence to recognise and further the standards and quality in their organisation. However, they must also have the necessary intuition and know how to achieve these goals through others.

Another approach of this particular school is based very much on leaders adapting their style to meet the situation in which they find themselves. This can apply to both organisational movements and other peoples capabilities

THE FUNCTIONAL APPROACH TO LEADERSHIP

This approach very much concentrates on the actions a leader must take to be successful. From this standpoint of concentrating on the leadership functions of management, different schools have arisen. Each of these schools seek to encapsulate a range of activities within a model.. A common form of this model and one of the most established and practical is the idea that a leader exists to do a job through the efforts of individuals working as a team. From this model springs the notion of three interrelated areas of work:

* Ensuring that required tasks are continually achieved

* Building and reinforcing a team

* Developing each individual member of the team.

It is this approach that I will be dwelling on. The functiona approach leads to more concrete outcomes and the successes o the approach can be measured more clearly.

THE FUNCTIONAL APPROACH ELABORATED

Companies in search of excellence, and that is an awful lot o companies nowadays, base their approach on three areas o work. Each area is intrinsically bound up with the other. Thes are:

* Achievement of tasks

* Teambuilding and development

* Individual development

There is a very simple model of action centered leadership seer overleaf.

If we look closely at the leader as part of the broader team then i can be seen that the leader is not actually a member of a tearr but is part of a level, or group with a longer timespan o horizons, greater levels of responsibility and more significan decision making power, which is part of greater responsibility and which have a greater impact on others. The effective leader will take one step back and be evaluating the outcomes and progress of team effort and will take the most appropriate action based on what the outcomes are. Sometimes it may be necessary to become a part of a team to provide additional input. The greatest skill a leader must have and exercise here is the ability to stand back at given times so as not to be accused of interfering. This is the difference between support and control.

ACTION CENTERED LEADERSHIP

ACHIEVEMENT OF TASKS

The fundamental duty of any manager, and thus leader is quite simple-on the face of it. *This is to accomplish the tasks for which the team and organisation exists.* It is vital then to be very clear what the objectives are. Too many organisations lose sight of their objectives, particularly when they grow. When the organisation loses sight of its goals then so do its managers. Therefore, they are weakened as leaders. This leads to discontent and gives people reason to criticize.

The team exists as a group and through teamwork it is the leaders responsibility to direct each individuals efforts towards the achievement of the organisations objectives. This is why they should be clear and realisable. A group of people can drift along for ever. However, the real aims and objectives of the organisation will not be realised in this case. The basic work may be done but excellence will not be achieved.

Teams will obviously differ in their individual makeup However, the leader has to identify the dynamics of individuals and the collective result and direct that energy to the desired end

This is one of the true tests of the intelligent leader. Someone who has the ability to stand back and assess each individual member of the team, to place that person within a wider frame and to identify appropriate tasks allied to these qualities, with the end result of the collective endeavor being the attainment of goals.

We will be looking more closely at teamwork a little later. It is obvious that teamwork is crucial to the success of any leader and the leader, the intelligence and disposition of that person, is crucial to the functioning of a successful team.

THE INDIVIDUAL IN THE TEAM

One of the key tasks of the leader, which will be elaborated on later is *valuing the individual.* This involves rewarding the person for his or her effort. It can also, unfortunately, involve the exercise of sanctions against an individual also. Ideally, every job should draw the best out of a person and must provide challenges for that person and the chance to achieve and be rewarded for that achievement. If a person begins to "mark time" and loses interest in the job then that individual can become a liability and will need managing in the negative sense. People can work but they are not really working in the true sense of the word and they certainly are not achieving.

Therefore, building a team, developing an individual and achieving tasks are all very much interrelated and fundamental to any leader. However, in the day to day operating environment the leader of people has to juggle with conflicting demands and to prioritize. It could be for example that the leader is under pressure to achieve a task. In this case it is vital that when the period of pressure is over the leader takes a back seat and reassesses the overall impact, both on the team and individuals.

Poor leadership can also be seen through over identification with one area of activity. Such a person might be driven or obsessed by figures and strive to achieve results on the basis of headline indicators. However, by doing this other key areas, such as people development, can be neglected.

In addition to the leader who is driven by figures, there is the person who wants to be popular with other team members. However, when this happens the leaders ability to take difficult decisions is eroded. Not all decisions are popular. To try to be popular is therefore a mistake and can lead to erosion of leadership abilities, power and confidence. As a word of warning, to try to be unpopular can have a negative effect also. To try too hard to be anything is a mistake when it comes to leadership. The key factor is recognition of the importance of the three elements of team, individual and task, to be sensitive to the work environment but at the same time to be seen as decisive and strong. We will be exploring the leader as decision maker a little later.

There is also the leader who will favour and concentrate on a few individuals in a team to the detriment of others. Invariably, this will happen and jealousy and disillusionment will arise fairly quickly. This is classic group reaction. A great deal of attention needs to be paid to this area and a true leader needs to be a sensitive leader. Without sensitivity then the process of demoralisation can occur.

THE PROCESSES OF LEADERSHIP

There are certain stages in the process of leadership. We have already talked about most of these stages in the previous pages. However, we need to elaborate a little further:

* *Definition of objectives.* This entails, as we have seen, being very clear about what the objectives of the team are. The objectives of a team of people will be bound up with the objectives of the organisation, which also need to be crystal clear;

* *Planning.* Planning, or a strategic approach, is absolutely necessary in order to achieve objectives. This involves several stages-the gathering of information and decision taking. When the gathering of information is over then so is the initial or consultative stage and the focusing on the task in question has to occur.

* *Briefing*-communicating the plan and the vision. It is essential that all are clear as to what is expected of them. Monitoring and support during the processes is also crucial.

* *Evaluation of the processes.* This requires constant evaluation

* *Re-evaluation and modification.* See overleaf for the action cycle (fig 2).

This cycle represents both small tasks and more major objectives. In developing the leadership process for a major task or project, constraints may be identified at an early stage without ever reaching the briefing stage. Similarly, having planned, we might be briefing the team when, as a result of questioning, it becomes clear that some aspect of the plan is very flawed. It could be argued that should have been identified during the gathering of information and consultative processes. Whatever, this process, or processes must be carefully planned and the outcome must be the clear result of being aware of each of the stages.

It is by following these leadership actions of defining the objectives, consulting, deciding, briefing, followed by support and monitoring and evaluation, that the manager is identified as a leader.

ACTION CYCLE

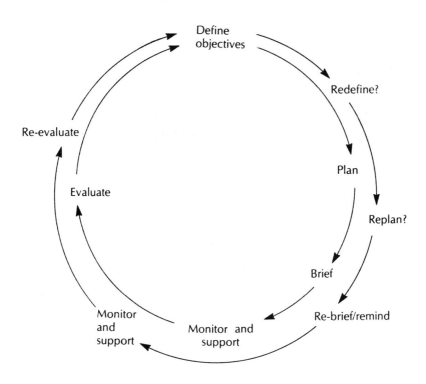

KEY POINTS FROM CHAPTER ONE

The following represent the key points from chapter one. However, they also elaborate on each area-the leaders main role in achieving tasks, in developing the team and developing individuals. The key points read almost as a checklist.

A leader has to be quite **CLEAR** about what the **TASK** is:

* The leader needs to communicate the task. However, the leader must also be clear his or herself about the task and how they fit into the objectives of the organisation

* The leader must plan to accomplish the task, define and provide the necessary resources needed

* The leader must understand and shape the organisational structure to ensure tasks can be completed more efficiently. Progress along the way must be charted and the results must be evaluated..

A leader must **BUILD a TEAM**

* Set and maintain objectives

* Communicate regularly with the team at least once a month, in a structured way, on matters of people, policy and points for action

* Consult with the team before taking decisions which affect them

* Communicate any changes taking place in the organisation and how they will affect the team

A leader must **DEVELOP INDIVIDUALS**

* Set targets and review them at regular intervals

* provide relevant training

* Group tasks to use people skill to the fullest

* Rotate jobs to broaden experience.

Make **PEOPLE FEEL VALUED**

* Know their name, place of work and other interests

* Regularly monitor efforts of people and provide feedback

* Be approachable

* Ensure that everyone understands the importance of their contribution to the organisation and also the function of the organisation.

* Recognise peoples achievements

* Hold regular meetings with each individual

The Leader must **EVALUATE PROGRESS**

* Are the objectives being achieved? If so, are there any individual or team contributions to acknowledge?

* In the event of success, do you acknowledge it and build on it, do you criticize constructively and give guidance on improving future performance?

* Design jobs and arrange work to make the best use of peoples skills and abilities. Continuously monitor this.

* Delegate effectively. Review tasks in the light of this.

* Set targets for individuals and measure them regularly

* Be sensitive to the welfare of the team and seek to improve working conditions

* In particular, provide leadership training to team leaders and potential leaders.

TO SUMMARISE

The job of a leader is to:

* get the required results (achieve task)

* Build an effective team

* Grow and develop each individual

Monitor and regularly evaluate progress.

Now turn to Chapter Two-Leadership through team building

EFFECTIVE LEADERSHIP

TEAM BUILDING

TEAM BUILDING

CHAPTER TWO

STAGE ONE-LEADERSHIP THROUGH TEAMBUILDING

In chapter One we discussed, very generally, the role of the team and the individual in relation to the activities of the leader. It is now time to look a little more closely at the Team within a working environment and how the functioning of a team is crucial to the overall success of an effective leader.

The first thing that we need to examine is the idea of a team, or what is a team. There are many notions and broad ideas put forward of the role of the team within the culture of an organisation. At its simplest, there is the idea that a team is a group of people working towards a common objective. However, people do not simply work towards a common objective. Both the organisation and leaders within the organisation have to develop certain elements for individuals within a team, *a sense of direction, a sense of belonging and a sense of identity.* It is certainly not good enough to let a group of people get on with defined tasks and somehow expect them to operate as a team.

A sense of direction is the overall vision of the external operating environment. This is commonly put forward by a mission statement, which we will be discussing in more detail later on. One very important cornerstone of a mission statement however, is that it should be underpinned by the organisations values, its culture. If it is not then it is worthless and will be more likely to promote cynicism than a sense of direction.

A sense of belonging will flow from a clear mission statement. The sense of belonging to an organisation flourishes as its members:

- Know what needs to be done
- Have the confidence in themselves and each other to do it
- Enjoy the process

A sense of identity will arise naturally from a high performance team which enables people to become aware of their individuality and recognise self worth and raise self confidence.

A sense of direction, belonging and identity are central to all teams. The task of the leader and the organisation is crucial in fostering this culture and climate.

THE TEAM AND ORGANISATIONAL CULTURE

Types of culture within organisations tend to stem from several different origins. The first is the corporate culture, promoted by an organisation as the general patterns of beliefs that are known understood and shared by most people in the organisation. However, the underpinning culture in an organisation is far less recognisable, or tangible. This is the overall willingness of the individual to accept and to "buy into" the corporate culture. This willingness is affected by a number of factors, not least their own past experience with an organisation and also their future ambitions.

Other factors to be considered are the power structures in the organisations and the activities of key individuals within those power structures. Unfortunately many managers rush around thinking that all before them will be loyal and devoted employees. However, this has more to do with ego and ambition than the actual reality. This reality sees a build up of resentment and an unwillingness of a team member to follow the leader. Therefore, it is crucial for the leader to concentrate on their own activities at all times and to ensure that others are not being ridden over rough shod.

In some organisations, the role culture is a key part of the overall corporate culture which affects peoples willingness to be led. The role culture works by logic and rationality and needs to be strong and identifiable. The role culture represents the pillars of the organisation and rests on procedures for roles, i.e. job descriptions, authority levels etc. and also procedures for communication. These are coordinated at the top by a narrow band of senior managers. Organisations which tend to develop dominant role cultures are usually large bureaucracies or other large organisations which operate in relatively stable environments where there is little sudden change. The downside of this type of culture is that it leads very clearly to departmentalization, leading to a lack of common vision and the inability to make decisions without referring those decisions upwards. The more management layers there are in place the more difficult it is to take instantaneous decisions, the more fearful people become and the less effective becomes the leader.

Although many more cultures arise within an organisation, depending on its size and structure and also history it is the above two that I wish to keep in focus as they are the two most likely to affect the ability of a leader to lead effectively-the culture of power and its corrosive effect on the morale of others and also the role culture inherent in a big bureaucracy.

Before you commit yourself to teamworking, and to shaping and fashioning a team it is necessary to stop and look at the nature of your organisation and to ask yourself:

* Which approach is prevalent in your organisation?
* Are there changes that need to be made?
* What are those changes?
* How can you make them

It could be that you are powerless to make the changes that you see as desirable. In this case, you need to look at the external inhibiting factors and to adopt an approach to your team which will work with the organisation but at the same time will achieve the desired results through your own vision. Remember, the effective leader is a person who will be looked up to precisely because he or she is effective.

Team development

The vast body of research which has been carried out into teamwork has demonstrated that teams have a dynamic of their own. They grow and develop and go through several stages on the way-each stage with its own distinctive characteristics.

There are several models of team development, one of the best known being **Tuckmans.**

Tuckmans model puts forward the four concepts of:

- *Forming*
- *Storming*
- *Norming*
- *Performing*

Therefore, he is putting forward four stages of team development.

Forming

Distinct and recognisable features of the forming stage are:

- At work, leaders of teams are nearly always appointed to take over existing or established teams

- Leaders rarely have the chance to select and build their own teams

- The initial adjustment period is often difficult

- Leaders try to stamp their authority whilst teams assess them

- Acceptance or rejection of leaders depends on whether the team will accept and follow them

- Many leaders will try to bolster their own egos by status symbols

- Winning the respect of members takes time and effort. Remember, when we are talking of peoples own positions in the company, their perceptions can be colored by many different factors

In the forming stage there are a number of crucial actions which need to be undertaken by a leader. It is crucial that those in the process get to know and assess each other. The function and purpose of the team needs to be collectively examined and an appraisal of the skills, knowledge and cohesiveness undertake, with an identification of the blocks present.

Storming

Recognisable features of the storming stage are:

- Feelings begin to come out into the open

- Team is focused on inner conflicts

- Team copes poorly when real pressure comes

- Team may have an unrealistic view of its own effectiveness

Development actions

- Debate risky issues

- Consider wider options

- Encourage wider openness and feedback

- Handle conflict positively

Norming

Recognisable features of the norming stage are:

- Ground rules are established

- Working procedures are agreed

- There is a high level of concern for a methodical approach to the task

- Closer working relations develop which are based on mutual trust and respect

- There develops an ability to discuss and deal with problems and conflicts in an objective way.

Development actions

- Maintain openness. This is crucial

- Review teams regularly

- Encourage challenges to established ways of doing things

- Celebrate successes

- Focus on individual as well as team effort

Performing

Recognisable features of the performing stage are:

- High flexibility

- Commitment to team goals

- Problem solving approach

- Conflicting views are handled positively and constructively

- Participative leadership

- Group synergy is achieved

The leader should recognise that teams are never static and once the performing stage has been reached it is vital to keep the team process under regular review to ensure that you stay there.

There are, of course, other models of team development. Another model is that put forward by W.R.Blon. Blon put forward the idea that teams not only go through stages of development but that team behaviour is also affected towards one another and the external environment. Blon identified four stages:

- *Dependency*

Where the team behaves as if its members were incapable of making decisions for themselves so that they look for strong directional leadership and expect the leader always to be the one to take the initiative.

- *Fight/Flight*

Where the team behaves as if it is under threat internally or externally. It begins to recognise other problems than that of authority, however, it is not ready to deal with them. It is at this particular stage that a team may draw together and overreact to a perceive threat. from elsewhere, or alternatively, in fighting can occur.

- *Pairings*

Where individuals begin to offer support to one another in pairs or sub groups. The team will then behave as if the impact of pairings or sub groups is highly influential in the life of the team.

- *Maturity*

This is where the team is fully developed. It can produce effective work and can deal with its emotional problems without threatening its stability.

It is fairly obvious that no model can adequately explain the dynamics of a particular team. They do however provide the leader with an opportunity to reflect on the team, the importance of the role of the team. The leadership role adopted towards a team in one stage of its formation will clearly not be the role needed for another stage. The effective leader should be fully aware of this and of the different stages of development.

Understanding the ways that teams develop, helping your team to move through the various stages and carrying out regular reviews can make a significant impact on the effectiveness of your team and also of the effectiveness of the leader.

Now read the key points from chapter two.

KEY POINTS FROM CHAPTER TWO

- The **FUNCTIONING** of a **TEAM** is crucial to the overall success of a leader

- **ORGANISATIONS** and **LEADERS** within the organisation have to develop certain elements for individuals within a team, a sense of **BELONGING,** a sense of **IDENTITY**, a sense of **DIRECTION**

- Teams are affected by particular **ORGANISATIONAL CULTURES,** in particular power structures and role cultures.

- Teams go through a number of different **STAGES** of DEVELOPMENT the most popular being those put forward by **TUCKMAN** and **BLON**

THE EFFECTIVE LEADER MUST PAY PARTICULAR ATTENTION TO THE PROCESS OF TEAM BUILDING.

NOW TURN TO Chapter Three stage two-The leader and delegation

DELEGATION

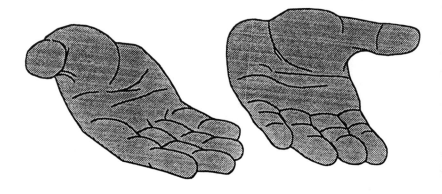

CHAPTER THREE

STAGE TWO-THE LEADER AND DELEGATION

Now we have considered management and leadership generally and also the initial process of team building, which is crucial to the strategy of the effective leader, we should consider the next stage, delegation.

Delegation is one of the most crucial aspects of a managers job. Without effective delegation, effective leadership cannot be achieved. Delegation is distinct from "giving out work" in that when a manager delegates you deliberately choose to give one of your staff authority to carry out a piece of work which could have been retained and done by yourself.

It is important to distinguish between responsibility, authority and accountability when looking at the meaning of delegation:

* *Responsibility,* in the context of delegation, means the work that is delegated-the task, job and duty

* *Authority* means the power to make decisions and take action, to enable this responsibility to be successfully discharged

* *Accountability* means "carrying the can" for the responsibility concerned-being held to account for the success or failure.

Successful delegation means matching responsibility with authority. To give a person responsibility without authority is certain to end in failure. Accountability is different in that managers are accountable for everything that goes on in their department. Therefore, delegation cannot take away your own ultimate accountability.

ADVANTAGES OF DELEGATION

Delegation enables the manager to concentrate on the more pressing aspects of a job, aspects which specifically require experience, skills and knowledge which you possess. Delegation frees up time which can be used to plan for the future and also does wonders for morale. Good delegation, or effective delegation breeds co-operation as staff see it as recognition of their capability. In addition, delegation is also an effective way of training staff to take on greater responsibility and to develop personally.

Although there are many advantages of delegation there are also disadvantages. There is an element of risk in that the person may be inexperienced. You can minimize the risk by planning delegation carefully. We will discuss this a little later.

There is also the difficulty of letting go of certain duties which you as manager might enjoy performing. In order to manage, and lead, effectively, then you have to let go and identify those tasks which can be effectively delegated. There is a classic syndrome where a manager will prefer to do everything because if it is not done then there is the fear that it never will be done. This leads to over control at the centre of operations and loss of motivation on the part of other staff. An effective leader is a person who can delegate and create the feeling of trust and confidence, but still retain overall control.

All managers, and consequently, effective leaders must delegate. The first thing that must be done is for the manager to look at his or her self and check for symptoms of failure to delegate The following represent personal symptoms of under delegating:

Do you have to take work home with you every night, or almost every night?

Do you work longer hours than those you are responsible for?

Are you frequently interrupted because others come to you with questions or for advice or decisions?

Do you spend some of your working time doing things for others which they could do for themselves?

Do you have unfinished jobs accumulating, or difficulty meeting deadlines?

Do you spend more of your time working on details as opposed to planning for the future?

Do you work at details because you enjoy them, although someone else could do them well enough?

Do you lack confidence in your staffs abilities so that you are afraid to risk letting them take on more responsibility?

Are you too conscientious about details that are not important for the main objectives of the job in hand?

Do you keep details secret from staff, so that one of them will not be able to displace you?

Do you believe that an executive should be rushed in order to justify his salary?

Do you hesitate to admit that you need help to keep on top of your job?

Do you neglect to ask staff for their ideas about problems that arise in their work?

Above are a list of classic symptoms which arise from lack of delegation. You should look at each on in turn and then ask yourself why the situation exists and what you are going to do about it. This is the beginning of your own personal plan and the beginning of effective management and leadership.

To delegate properly you must have a plan. You should write down the main objectives of your job and ensure that your job description is accurate and up to date. Main objectives are not numerous. They specify ends rather than means. You need to look at your diary for the last month and analyze how you spent your time. This will start to reveal a pattern of what you do.

You should draw up a basic chart based on the information revealed. This provides a comparison between stage one (objectives) and stage two (actual activities)

At this point you should be ready to decide what can be delegated. It is important to recognise areas which cannot be delegated:

* Tasks well beyond the skills and experience of your staff

* Confidential, security and policy matters which are restricted to your own level of seniority

* Matters involving exercising discipline over the individuals peers.

When checking items against this list, make sure that you are not using it as a means of rationalizing your reluctance to delegate. Having ruled out items which fit with the criteria above you should still be left with a range of possible tasks to delegate. The first two areas to look at are routine tasks, and tasks consuming a lot of your own time.

Routine tasks are good delegation material. What is routine to you as a manager will be new to someone below you and by delegating you will be stretching and developing that member of staff and giving yourself more time to concentrate on more crucial areas.

Tasks consuming a lot of your time provide obvious delegation opportunities. This is especially true if the reason that they are time consuming is either that you are not very good at them or you have simply run out of new ways of tackling them. Someone else may come up with a quicker and better method. After taking into account the above you should be in a position to produce a detailed delegation plan for one or more of your staff.

Having reached the stage where you have identified certain tasks you wish to delegate, you now have to consider both how and to whom they are going to be passed on. This can be done by analyzing each of your staff in turn, thinking through these questions:

* What skills, qualifications and experience does that person have which are currently being used and not being used?

* What type of work have they shown an interest in but has not yet done?

* What type of work could they not do adequately in spite of further training?

The answers to the above should help you decide who is the appropriate person to take on each item of delegated responsibility. You can then complete your delegation program.

You will want to discuss this with the person concerned. If you are already operating a system of target setting, this discussion should take place at each review. The form that the discussion takes will depend partly on the reason for choosing a particular person.

In accepting a newly delegated responsibility, the person must be clear about three constraints on the way they handle it. These are:
* Objectives

* Policies

* Limits of authority.

Many duties can be delegated progressively. Very few can be handed over straight away in a single step. It is important, when you have delegated a task to an individual that you also notify the people who will be affected, especially those in other departments whose co-operation may be needed in order to achieve the task.

DELEGATION AT SENIOR LEVELS

For all organisations, the higher the management level, the more you should be concerned with planning the future and the less with organising day to day problems. What employees look for from a manager is a clear plan for the future.

Making strategy is not something that can be delegated. Staff at all levels should be involved in some way in the planning process but strategy decisions based on these plans have to be taken at a higher level. Therefore, day to day management, as much a possible, should be delegated to more junior levels in order to free up time for strategic planning.

One other key function of the senior manager is that of dealing with, or shaping, the external environment. The external environment has a direct impact on all business and senior managers have to be in a position to be able to recognise and absorb any changes, for example, in legislation, that may have an impact on the core business.

DEVELOPING OTHER MANAGERS

It is crucial that managers are developed, particularly if they are to take over key roles in the organisation. A useful device for this is to arrange for a manager to shadow or cover someone else in order to learn the basics of their job. This widens that persons horizons and goes a long way to preparing him or her for more responsibility in a senior post.

WALKING THE JOB

It is essential that, having delegated tasks to others you see how they are performing for yourself. Walking the job is a very effective way indeed. In this way too you can be visible and not locked away and rarely seen, as is the lot of many.

DEALING WITH MISTAKES

Delegation involves taking a calculated risk and in spite of careful preparation you will sometimes find that individuals make mistakes. How people respond to mistakes depends on the manager in question, on the person delegated to and the nature of the mistake.

If the individual has made a mess of the job through lack of planning, then some patient coaching from yourself is probably called for. It could be that the person doing the job has lost confidence and cannot continue with the task. You will need to talk this over carefully with the manager concerned and pin down the problems and find a solution.

It could be that it has turned out that the person has not measured up to the responsibility. You will need to judge whether or not that person needs more training, or whether it is time to cut your losses and take that particular task away from him.

Throughout the process of analyzing mistakes, it is helpful to keep two points in the forefront:

* Everyone makes mistakes and as long as they are not the result of stupid behaviour then there is little to be ashamed of

* Mistakes can be used as an opportunity to learn.

Even when mistakes are not being made with delegated tasks, the manager has a responsibility for control. The spot check is perhaps the simplest method to use. After the job holder has carried out his task a couple of times, you can check on how it is going. If the task involves much liaison with another department, have a quiet word with the departmental head and ask how the person is handling it. If the task involves written work, ask to see a copy of the report concerned. If it is running a committee, ask one of the committee members how the meetings are going.

If you have successfully delegated a task, there is a lot for you yourself to learn. The following questions should be asked:

* Has the job holder found a new way of performing the task, which can be copied elsewhere?

* Are there any other tasks which you are handling yourself which you could now delegate?

* Has success here stimulated others of your team to want more responsibility?

* Can you learn anything about the training period needed to perform this sort of task?

* Have you made sure about updating your own and the other persons job description to transfer the responsibility?

How much of your time has now been saved and how are you using it? Can you improve your own coaching responsibility so that other tasks can be delegated more easily from now on?

Having delegated a task, it is only too easy for the time saved to be wasted and you may end up with a feeling that "delegation does not pay". Evaluating the results of delegation should reassure you that it does pay.

Once the task really does belong to the post holder and you have confidence to let him get on with it, what should you do next?

At this stage, you can rely on what is known as "management by exception". This means that you assume that standards are being met unless told otherwise. No news is good news and you do not have masses of paperwork to deal with. Such reports as you do get will highlight deviations from the norm and you can concentrate your attention on these.

Obviously, you cannot manage totally by exception and some degree of control will directly relate to the nature of the task. However, in most cases you can and if there is no negative feedback then it can be assumed that all is proceeding relatively smoothly.

SUMMARY

Delegation is not easy. It takes hard work and not a little effort. However, the manager who fails to delegate is no manager. The manager who fails to delegate is not an effective leader. The effective leader is a person who has command of the knowledge of what is needed in order to create a dynamic and effective operational culture. The person who can create this can inspire confidence, the confidence that a good manager needs and, in turn, a leader needs in order to be effective.

Now turn to the Key points from chapter three, stage two.

KEY POINTS FROM CHAPTER THREE, STAGE TWO

- **DELEGATION** is one of the most crucial areas of a managers job. Without **EFFECTIVE DELEGATION**, effective leadership cannot be achieved.

- It is important to distinguish between **RESPONSIBILITY, AUTHORITY** and **ACCOUNTABILITY** when looking at the meaning of delegation

- **DELEGATION** enables the manager to concentrate on the more pressing aspects of a job

- To delegate properly you must have a **PLAN**

- It is important to recognise areas which **CAN** and **CANNOT** be delegated.

Now turn to Chapter four, stage three, the leader and the decision making process

EFFECTIVE LEADERSHIP

THE DECISION MAKING PROCESS

EFFECTIVE LEADERSHIP

CHAPTER FOUR

STAGE THREE-THE LEADER AND THE DECISION MAKING PROCESS

Having considered management and leadership, team building and delegation, we must now look at the importance of the decision making process in the overall strategy of the effective leader.

Along with the increasing rate of change in the workplace is the increasingly high level of expectation of people at work. The need for managers to manage by ability and not by status is more pressing than ever before and this has resulted also in a far more open style of management and leadership. The leader has to create the environment which encourages people to make use of their skills to the common value of the organisation. This can no longer be done through coercion alone.

People have to be involved in the decision making process. However, by doing this there is the underlying fear that management will lose the initiative. We need to understand very clearly that the process of decision taking involves people in a manner which contributes to the effectiveness of the decision and its implementation without undermining the vital leadership role of an individual leader. What, therefore, we must develop is the ability to combine the many skills that encapsulate the manager as a leader, in being an effective decision taker.

STAGES OF DECISION TAKING.

The art of effective leadership is in making difficult things simple. In relation to the leader and the decision making process, it needs to be understood that decision making is based on five principle stages:

* **CONSIDER**. Define the objective and consider the problem

* **CONSULT**. The stage at which you take initiatives to involve those affected. This is of the utmost importance

* **COMMIT**. Ensuring that appropriate action will be taken.

* **COMMUNICATE**. The stage at which you explain what has been decided and why.

* **CHECK**. The need for visible leadership in ensuring the decision actually works.

This is the foundation on which the leader can build more detailed actions. However, the stages cannot always be based on a progressive step by step process. Sometimes it is necessary to go back a stage and repeat part of the loop. For example, following consultation with others and establishing further facts, it becomes clear that we need to return to the initial question or problem and reconsider the objective. Consultation may not be applicable or appropriate in all situations. Through reason of policy or emergency the manager may skip the consultation stage, as a matter of necessity.

There is no recognition of negotiation in the above stages. This is because negotiation is a separate stage when no leader has the authority to take the decision. When that authority does exist, we must ensure that neither "consult" nor "communicate" degenerate into negotiation. It is vital that we either have one person taking the decision and being accountable, or a joint party negotiating. In either event, consultation before meeting at the negotiating table is important, as are the communication processes that would follow. During negotiation, however, we have more than one organisation system conducting these two stages (e.g., management seeking view and explaining outcome, whilst union officials or employee representatives would be doing likewise).

Overleaf Fig 3 demonstrates the decision making process and key actions.

Fig 3 Decision making and key actions

Consider	Consult	Commit	Communicate	Check
Ultimate objective	Others likely to be affected	A plan of action within time scale	Face-to-face in teams	Decision is being implemented Walk the job
ESTABLISH Problems Cause and effect Who is affected Time scales Constraints	ENCOURAGE Attendance Suggestions Listening Creativity Time to think	Take the decision Write it down Be committed and enthusiastic	EXPLAIN Sell the decision Check understanding	EVALUATE Understanding and acceptance Training Standards Quality Delegation Rewards Is it achieving the objective?

What, Why, When, Who, Where, How.

KEY ACTIONS FOR DECISION TAKING

Regardless of the complexity of the decision it is vital to be clear at the outset who will ultimately take that decision. Managers are more enthusiastic about carrying out decisions that they have taken themselves. However, it is much more practical to delegate decision taking as far down the line as possible.

There are enormous rewards to be gained from trusting people rather than not trusting them, with all the accompanying problems of time, failing initiative and morale, and enjoying the (false) luxury of being indispensable. We are all dispensable.

It is incumbent on leaders at every level to think carefully about the following actions and to be continually looking for ways to improve and open up the decision making process.

CONSIDER

The decision making process starts when it is apparent that some management action or initiative is necessary. The first action is to give yourself time to think. Consider if the real problem is being tackled and not merely the superficial symptoms of an underlying factor, or indeed, whether intervention is really necessary. Some problems solve themselves without the need for outside help. In some circumstances the best decision is to take no decision. Next, however, you should consider what your aim is, what do you want to achieve.

67

Establish what information is needed and how to get it. Consider the nature of the decision, the constraints and the time scales.

Establish a checklist

* Has the real problem been defined?

* What is the decision intended to achieve?

* By when must the decision be taken?

* What other constraints are there?

* What would be the effect if no decision were taken?

* what information is needed?

* Should it be delegated?

CONSULTATION

Experience has demonstrated that group decision taking is not usually practical. The collective approach usually gets the decision takers bogged down. Not in all cases, but in most. However, at the same time, the other extreme, no consultation at all breeds lack of commitment. The most effective way of involving people is to adopt the approach of consultation before decision. In this way people are involved.

To illustrate the point of consultation and commitment, one only has to look at the history of post war housing, in the 30 years following the end of the second world war.

Peoples access to public housing was tightly controlled, as it is today. However, people were channeled into environments and management of their communities, or at least key decisions, took place around them. Over the years this has led to a fundamental lack of respect for environments, a culture of bars against doors and graffiti on walls, of violence and loathing for local and national politicians.

This is primarily because, along the way people were not involved in the key decision making processes which went on around them and felt no part of what was happening. The result is a lack of commitment and lack of sense of belonging which has led to a downward spiral.

Although this example is dramatic, lack of consultation within teams of people who are acting within the framework of objectives can lead to lack of commitment and disinterest. It is crucial that people are involved in the processes of decision making and that leaders involve their teams in the key stages.

Consultation can be limited to the immediate workgroup, as is the case with operational decisions. However, some tactical and strategic decisions affect far wider areas of the organisation and different mechanisms for consultation may be used, such as unions etc.

The timing of consultation will often call for sensitivity and good judgement. There is a strong case for consulting as early as is possible, so as to allow time for people to weigh up the pro's and con's of the situation. This needs to be weighed up against the need to avoid long drawn out and possibly destructive discussions of contentious issues. Whatever, it is necessary to set a time limit so that everyone knows when consultation stops and a decision be taken.

The following should be observed:

* Have all the people who should be consulted been identified?

* Has the information which should be tabled, including the constraints, been assembled?

* Have meetings been convened of consultative committees and trade union representatives?

* Has the timing of consultation been chosen with care and a date been set for concluding the process?

* Have you attempted to think outside the problem by creating a task force and using creative techniques such as brainstorming?

* Are you fully prepared to listen to ideas and suggestions without jumping to conclusions?

COMMIT

Having been through the first two stages, it is now necessary to take a decision. A number of things can and do go wrong here:

* Insufficient time to think at the first stage, being under pressure or quite simply getting on and acting, omitting to consult generally

* Failing to listen at stage two, either not consulting at all or doing it in such a way that you were not really receptive to the others in the process

* Failing to assemble sufficient relevant data at stage two or assembling so much that important issues were not given priority because they were not clear

* Failing to face the issues within the timescales set for action, and not progressing beyond stage two.

When you eventually make the decision it is often the case that it is not an ideal one in the circumstances. The cardinal rule is that the leader must be seen to be making a decision. It may not be the right one at the end of the day. However, it is not always possible to make the perfect decision when quite often the nature of the operating environment quite often means that whatever you do will result in a certain degree of unpopularity and dissent. However, once taken, stick by your decision.

COMMUNICATION

Poor communications lead to inadequate decision making processes and ultimately to decisions floundering. It is absolutely necessary to secure peoples commitments to decisions by communicating face to face. It is necessary to sell decisions, explaining the decision and giving people an opportunity to ask questions. Other methods of communication, noticeboards and memo's for example, are back up methods but cannot take the place of face to face communication.

It is the job of the person taking the decision to ensure that they communicate. Managers who are leaders will not avoid this process of face to face communication.

Team briefing is a very convenient way of transmitting decisions and ensuring that all are informed by the team leader. The crucial point is to explain the decisions, the reason for them and when the decision is expected to be implemented.

Clear communication can reduce peoples fear of change and also effectively combats rumor, which is a great source of insecurity.

You should check:

* Have the methods of implementing a decision been planned?

* Have all those affected been briefed in teams, with facts and reasons face to face?

* Are the channels to feedback fully understood?

* Have all those affected accepted the decision?

MONITORING

There is a need to know whether the decision you have taken is actually working. Although a great deal of information can be gained from statistics and other feedback, it is vitally important to walk the job, to observe the operation for which people are responsible and talking to people. We need to catch people "doing things right" and if the decision is not working then we need to review potential weak areas. These are:

* Inadequate information

* Poor judgment

* Lack of courage

* Inadequate plans for implementation

* A breakdown in briefing

* Lack of enthusiasm on the part of management.

You should evaluate whether:

* People have understood the briefing and accepted the implications

* Whether anyone needs training as a result of what is being actioned

* That standards are being achieved

* Whether quality can be improved

* Whether authority can now be delegated for subsequent decisions

* Is corrective action needed?

The effective leader must take decisions by drawing on other peoples skills and experiences whilst having the leadership responsibilities of deciding which course of action. That person must also have the drive and the commitment to see that course of action implemented.

Decision taking really draws on skills of communicating and effectiveness. An effective communicator is an effective decision maker, who is also an effective leader.

Now read the key points from chapter four, stage three.

KEY POINTS FROM CHAPTER FOUR

- People have to be **INVOLVED** in the decision making process

- The decision making process is based on five principle stages:

CONSIDER

CONSULT

COMMIT

COMMUNICATION

CHECKING

It is important to **MONITOR** whether decisions taking are actually working.

The effective leader must take decisions by drawing on other peoples skills and experience whilst having the leadership responsibility of deciding which course of action.

Now turn to chapter five, stage four, the leader and effective communications.

COMMUNICATIONS

CHAPTER FIVE

STAGE FOUR-THE LEADER AND EFFECTIVE COMMUNICATIONS

We are now at stage four. The importance of decision taking runs as a thread through the other areas that we have discussed. Now we need to consider communication generally, the ideal mediums of communication and relate these to the importance of effective leadership.

Failure to communicate can be very costly indeed. The leader must communicate and communicate well. We have seen, in the previous chapter that failure to communicate can lead to the collapse of the decision making process. When we are dealing with the process of change, the full benefits can only be achieved, and the process handled successfully, when people are communicated with.

People will also only give their best if they fully understand the decisions that affect them and the reasons behind those decisions. People should be clear about:

* What they have to do and why

* How they are performing

* What their conditions of employment are.

If people are involved in what they are doing then they will operate more efficiently and more willingly. It is up to the leader to ensure that there is clear communication on all levels. There is a need for a properly organised system of communication and also a clear set of priorities on what to communicate.

The priority is for the leader to communicate understanding of those matters that significantly affect a persons will to give the best of their work. People need to understand:

* What is the job?

* Who is the boss?

* What contribution does my work make to the total job?

* Where does the work come from and go to?

* What is the end product of my labors?

* What are the targets for work?

* To what extent can I influence costs?

* What are the safety standards?

* What is the rate of pay and how are my salaries or wages calculated?

* What are the holiday arrangements?

* What are my chances of promotion?

* What are the negotiating arrangements ?

* What changes are being made and why?

There are so many different strands to effective communication with people. A lot of those mentioned above are basic items of communication and should, in most cases, be given to people at the outset of their employment, either in written form, or induction or preferably both.

The effective leader has to have a clear idea of effective communication and should be familiar with three main methods in all forms of organisation:

* Face to face communication

* Communication through representatives

* Mass methods

Face to Face

The manager or supervisor, as the representative of management to the work group is the appropriate person to explain the most important matters we have discussed because these things result from managerial decisions or, in the case of negotiated matters, from joint management/union decisions.

Part of the job of being a leader is to be the person to whom people look to for explanations. By becoming a communicator the manager or supervisor will become a better leader.

Managers can tailor explanations to suit the particular group and, following the explanation, questions can be asked. What needs to be explained to one group will be different for another.

Much of what must be communicated is already common knowledge to the manager. For example, reasons for changes in production which will affect a persons job.

Face to face communication with the group saves time, ensures common understanding, and is the most powerful method of selling ideas and building group commitment.

There are of course weaknesses, in certain situations, with this method. With a line of leadership of more than two levels between the top manager and the person on the shop floor or in the office, communication by this method does not happen adequately unless organised. In addition, the line of leadership cannot alone handle adequately upward communication.

COMMUNICATION THROUGH REPRESENTATIVES

This provides an opportunity for management to explain a policy directly to a few of the employees affected, saving much repetition at different levels. The formal contact in meetings of this sort can and does bring an increase in informal contact and can help to create a bridge with senior management.

However, there are weaknesses with this form of communication. Many representatives often fail to explain the full import of decisions to other colleagues, particularly if the information to be passed on is unpleasant. Representatives are often put into impossible positions in that they often have to explain management's policies.

Finally, if shop stewards are the communicators they, and not the supervisors will become the leader of the workgroup.

MASS METHODS OF COMMUNICATION

Mass methods of communication offer the cheapest, but not the most effective way of giving information to large numbers of people. They can be quick and accurate. However, as with other forms of communication there are weaknesses. One main weakness is that they are fairly rigid and leave no room for discussion and there is also the problem of whether the information is accurately received. Mass methods can only cover matters very generally and cannot be specific. For a leader to be specific information needs to be communicated to groups as opposed to the mass.

When choosing a method of communication, you should recognise that any systematic method is better than none at all. The mass method is easier to work. The hardest is through managers and supervisors However, communication up and down will not be satisfactory in a large organisation without some use of all three methods. The most important task for a leader is to make communication work through managers and supervisors.

All members of management, including supervisors and foremen must be made to appreciate the importance and benefits of effective communication. Communication cannot be left to informal or ad hoc methods.

If communication down through line management is to be effective, it has to be systematic. The object is to ensure that employees have the decisions that affect their job or conditions of employment explained to them face to face by their immediate boss. Two steps are needed. Firstly establish a drill for team briefing that ensures communication right down the line to the work group, through supervisors. Secondly, ensure that the necessary information is known by managers.

TEAM BRIEFING

Team briefing is a systematic drill to ensure that communication takes place. The crucial element is that the information briefed to the group should be relevant to that group. The drill that ensures that this happens is that all briefers prepare the local items that need to be briefed, before receiving a briefing from their local manager. This ensures that, at each level, the brief from above is being added to an existing local brief.

Managers must decide when briefing sessions will be held. In the case of day workers , this is often done during the lunch hour. Shift workers may be brought in early or held late and paid overtime. Office or shop workers are briefed either first thing in the morning or just before closing time. The important thing is to ensure that everyone is included and that the brief is clear and unambiguous.

For briefing to be credible, it must be regular, with dates set systematically. This can tie in with the frequency of information. Subjects covered will be decisions and policies that affect peoples lives and their will to work. The four main headings in a briefing will tend to be:

* Progress (how you are doing)

* People

* Policy

* Points for action

* Forthcoming priorities.

Local matters will predominate at all levels.

The sessions should normally last not more than half an hour. Two thirds of this time should be spent explaining and one third listening. Normally the section head will take the briefing. Generally, people need to be experienced in:

* The skills of briefing others

* Writing a local brief

* Delivering the brief

* Handling questions and feedback

Systems should be monitored and a group should be formed to co-ordinate feedback to the briefing.

If a team briefing has not been the norm in the workplace then it will be necessary to put those most closely involved on a training course. The first few briefs should not contain controversial subjects.

MAKING BETTER USE OF EMPLOYEES KNOWLEDGE

As we have seen, effective communication of ideas and opinions upwards from employees to management is essential for all organisations seeking full efficiency. At one end of the scale is the system of representatives and the consultative committees. At the other is the local level problem solving team. Both types of consultation improve efficiency and increase the employers sense of involvement.

Direct discussions between employees and senior management are essential if managers are to be aware of the attitudes and feelings of those who will be affected by management decisions. Without such discussions, wrong decisions can result. Except in very small companies, some systematic committee meeting with elected representatives is necessary.

The purpose of a consultative committee is to give employees a chance to improve decisions by contributing comments before decisions are made and to make the fullest possible use of their experience and ideas in the running of the organisation. The consultative group is also the ideal forum to give managers and employers the opportunity to understand each others views and objectives at first hand.

The main function of a committee is to discuss, before any decisions are taken, any matter affecting the efficiency of the enterprise and the interests of employees to which representatives can contribute.

There should be no limitation on the subjects discussed with the exception of matters which are highly confidential or which are considered to be trade secrets, In addition, matters covered in union agreements if the committee is non union should not be discussed.

The following are examples of subjects which can be of concern to consultative committees:

* Output and productivity

* Manpower policies and procedures

* Education and training

* Safety

* Selection and training Of supervisors

* Effectiveness of communication.

In addition, a committee which is union based will be in a position to discuss, before negotiations take place:

* Wage systems

* Job Evaluation

* Hours of work

* Holidays and holiday pay

Agendas should be circulated in advance, with supporting information. More than half the agenda should be initiated by management. It is useful to have one major subject at each meeting. All agendas should include an item which allows the chairman to talk about the progress of works or office or department. This is not with a view to it being passed on, but to remind representatives of the organisational background against which they are talking.

There is no need to have an equal number of representatives from each side. A membership of not more than 16 will produce a good committee. If the firm recognises trade unions it is best to include shop stewards whenever possible.

Committees should meet about every two months if they are to be effective. And minutes should be prepared. Effective reporting back is very important indeed. It may be worthwhile considering the following when reporting back:

* A committee news sheet should be circulated immediately following the meeting.

* Allotted times for reporting back

* Management briefing of the decisions taken after consultation, stating that consultation has taken place.

MASS METHODS OF COMMUNICATION

Earlier, we talked about mass methods of consultation. The most effective mass methods are:

* Noticeboards

* Company magazines

* Annual reports

* Employees handbooks

* Loudspeaker systems

* Phone in arrangements

* Mass meetings

The location of noticeboards is very important. They should be where people regularly pass or stop. People should be made responsible for the maintenance of noticeboards and notices should be signed by individuals so that people have a direct recognition.

Company magazines or noticeboards should:

* Provide a mass means of explaining the companies activities and policies to its employees

* To help employees feel that they are involved in the company

* To create an atmosphere in which change is accepted

The emphasis, when planning company publications, should be on frequency and flexibility. Distribution should be carefully planned. Space in company newspapers should be divided into thirds: one third for the product and other news that affects a persons job; one third for developments or changes in conditions of employment and one third for social events.

Employees will receive an employees handbook when they start work, or should do. This sets out the main rules of the company and care should be taken to ensure that they are as friendly and accessible as possible.

Mass meetings

Mass meetings are valuable as the only practical way for people to hear the most senior managers directly. They are not good for getting understanding simply because people cannot ask questions. They are not a substitute for team briefing sessions.

The annual report

The annual report gives people an opportunity to understand the vital importance of their work and how it contributes to the whole. More and more companies issue a special report which sets out the main facts and provides the opportunity to ex[plain that:

* they have produced a certain volume of goods and services for other people, whatever they may be

* They have generated the incomes of those employed

* They have provided tax revenue

* They have generated savings in reserve for future development

* They have generated a return on peoples savings in distributed profits

Obviously, there is other useful information which can be passed on to employees. This very much depends on the nature type and situation of the company in question.

The effectiveness of the report depends on how it is distributed. It is best distributed in a meeting, or team briefing. This ensures that everyone receives the report and gets a chance to ask questions.

Other mass visual aids to communication are

* Posters

* Filmstrips and videos

All are most effective when they are used as an aid to face to face communication.

Written communications and other such methods can never become the main vehicle for communication. One of the dangers with inadequate communication is that it breeds remoteness and hostility.

The leader has to be aware of all different forms of communication and how to utilize them to their best effect.

CHECKING THAT COMMUNICATION IS WORKING

Walking the job is one of the most effective ways of checking on flows of communication. This can reveal whether or not a decision or fact has been communicated well or received at all.

Discussion through formal groups is also a very effective method of checking whether or not a certain item has been communicated and received.

In addition, depending on the size of your company, a questionnaire is a very effective way of receiving feedback.

Now read the key points from chapter five.

KEY POINTS FROM CHAPTER FIVE

The manager and, ultimately, the leader should consider the following crucial points when considering the importance of communication in the workplace and its role in ensuring that leadership is effective.

- Failure to communicate can be very costly indeed

- When we are dealing with the ongoing process of change, the full benefits can only be achieved when people are communicated to

- People will only give their best if they fully understand the decisions that affect them and the reasons behind those decisions

- If people are involved in what they are doing then they operate more willingly and efficiently

- There are many different strands to effective communication with people

- The effective leader should be familiar with three main methods of communication in all forms of organisation-face to face-communication through representatives and mass methods

- Team briefing is a very effective way of communicating

- The manager and thus effective leader should check that communication is working effectively

- Walking the job is one very effective way of monitoring communication

SUMMARY

EFFECTIVE LEADERSHIP

This book has adopted an unusual approach in that it has not exclusively concentrated on leadership theories but has tried to mix the fundamental principles of management in a busy environment with the concept of effective leadership. The approach has been very much on the attainment of leadership through teambuilding, delegating, decision making and general communication.

These processes, the human elements are very much at the forefront of day to day activity and take up a lot of a managers time. Or, should do.

One of the key problems is that by addressing the notion of the effective leader in isolation, outside of the working environment, we never really approach a synthesis of activities which, combined, can lead to a person becoming an effective leader of people.

Note that no assumptions are made about "born" leaders or "natural leaders" only the person attaining effective leadership through mastery of the processes which influence and drive people in the work environment.

Remember, you are dealing with people in a workplace. You are dealing with the manifestations of the human personality, both individually and combined and it is absolutely necessary to have a grasp, and be in control of, the processes which arise when groups of individuals interact together.

The final thesis of this book is that leaders can develop from able people who have an insight into the dynamics of the workplace.

Go forward and become an effective leader!

EFFECTIVE LEADERSHIP

STRAIGHTFORWARD GUIDES

If you have any comments concerning this book or are interested in writing for Straightforward, please contact:

Straightforward Publishing 38 Cromwell Road
London E17 9JN

Your views are appreciated.

Straightforward Publishing: authors writing for the community.

EFFECTIVE LEADERSHIP

Other Guides in the series:

A Straightforward Guide to

The Rights of the Private Tenant
Divorce and the Law
Computing
Teaching Your Child to Swim
Teaching Your Child to Read and Write
Small Claims in The County Court
Personal Finance
Accounts and Bookkeeping for Small Business
Leaseholders Rights
Taking Your Own Legal Action
Employment Law
Family Law
Creative Writing
Freelance Writing
Letting a Property for Profit-Landlords Guide
Getting the Best out of Your Solicitor
What to Expect When You go to Court
The Bailiff, the Law and You
Effective Leadership
Consumer Law
Buying and Selling a Home
Doing Your Own Conveyancing
Carrying out Your Own Structural Survey
Effective Negotiations

Public Speaking
Speech Writing
Self Defense for Disabled People

Guides without the Straightforward Guide Prefix

The Straightforward C.V
Marketing Explained
Caring For a Disabled Child
The Straightforward Business Plan
Century Guide to the 100 best Stately Homes
Century Guide to the 100 best Car Museums
Century Guide to 100 best Public Gardens
Century Guide to 100 best Steam Railway Experiences